To Bob —
with much
admiration for
your own flair
for lanvage. . .

Metaphors
Be
with
You

Bi. Ruck

June 1988
Bishop Ireton

Between a Rock and a Heart Place

Scripta humanistica

Directed by
BRUNO M. DAMIANI
The Catholic University of America

ADVISORY BOARD

Between a Rock and a Heart Place

Rick Wilson, T.O.R.

Scripta humanistica

43

Wilson, Rick, 1954
    Between a Rock and a Heart Place / by Rick Wilson.
        p. cm. — (Scripta Humanistica: 43)
    ISBN 0-916379-51-5: $25.00
    I. Title. II. Series: Scripta Humanistica (Series): 43.
PS3573.I4654B4   1987   88-1922
811'.54—dc19   CIP

            Publisher and Distributor:
            SCRIPTA HUMANISTICA
            1383 Kersey Lane
            Potomac, Maryland 20854 U.S.A.

        Printed in the United States of America

Acknowledgements

Grateful acknowledgement is made to the following publications and anthologies in which these poems or versions of them originally appeared: *Crossroads, Gargoyle, The Monocacy Valley Review, Phoebe: The Greoge Mason Review, Piedmont Literary Review, Pivot, Poet Lore, Poets On, Potomac Guardian Journal, St. Anthony Messenger, The Other Side, Unicorn, Virginia Writing, Visions,* **Whose Woods These Are** *(Word Works),* **Night House Anthology: 48 Younger American Poets** *(Four Zoas Press).*

The author is grateful to the Immaculate Conception Province of the Franciscan Friars, Third Order Regular, for their support and generosity which made this collection possible.

Contents

Foreword

To begin, I should point out that I am not a poet. Oh, I wanted to be, once, when I was twenty or so, and believed myself to be rather tragic, and possessed of the kind of sensitivity that poets had (this meant one was constantly thinking of death, and was constantly in love, and was, well, tortured a lot); what I suppose I wanted was for someone to say to *anyone* else that I was a poet. Then, I could carry the title around. Well, there is a wonderful line I heard somewhere—attributed, then, to the English—which goes like this: "When you're twenty and a poet, you're twenty; when you're thirty and a poet, you're probably a poet." In any case, while I am not a poet, I have remained an avid reader of poetry, and having pointed this out I'm afraid I must go on to say that an awful lot of poetry I see from people near my age (42) and younger, is limp, and seems to be suffering from a kind of near-sightedness, a species of cloying, self-absorbed, lyricism that leaves me cold. We have had the confessional poets, and the beat poets, and the glitter poets, and the poets of what some people call the disastrous generation—Plath, Lowell, Sexton, Berryman, Jarrell—and so on and so on, and now we have what has been called a return to formalism, this apparently spawning a particularly odd beast called the "well made poem of our time." And all of this in the hands of the poets of roughly my age has resulted in a strange lack of engagement with the world outside the self and the self's sordidness: too many of the poems I read these days are about the poet seeing the landscape in his own mind, and the poems themselves contain constellations of private symbologies that seem designed to keep an interested reader out—or to let him so far

1

in as to make him wish for some other kind of travel. And having said all this, I now hasten to point out that there are notable exceptions to the trend: Roland Flint, Henry Taylor, Dave Smith, Ai, Margaret Gibson and Michael Collier to name a few. Rick Wilson now joins the exceptions with this fine collection.

For while there is always a clearly sensed vision, a singular sensibility in these poems, there is also a palpable, fully realized world, where fish rise to the offered blessing of historical saints, where beer cans lie in autumnal shadow, or "Midsummer heat hangs / heavy as a confessional curtain on Saturday." This world is the real world, it is recognizable as the face of a friend or brother, but it is also, in the eyes of this poet, sentient, awake or heading for the state of being awake, and, in some way that the poet sometimes confesses not to understand—or, rather, sees as a thing wrapped in mystery and wonder—sanctified by the prsence of God.

> *Listen:*
> *The soft caress of unknowing,*
> *something*
> *that almost hints at prayer.*

But this is not a book that is particularly somber or intentionally mystical about these things, either—there is much humor here (I am especially fond of the found poem "Exeunt: A Collage of Their Last Lines," which is a brilliant arrangement of the purported last words of some of our revered and famous), and much anger, too (see particularly "The Alchemy of Pain" and "Time On Its Side,"). There is passion, ("Love Poem," and "Broken Sleep") and simple celebration ("Relief Map," "Sun Dance," "Nocturnal Benison," and "Winter Prelude"), and there are even some black jokes about the human predicament ("Exeunt" again, and "Granuloma"). And, for those who pay more attention to such things, this variety of experience and tone is reflected in matters of technique and approach: each poem takes its own form, assumes its own voice and manner and shape, without ever seeming facile, or affected, or merely a matter of form. In short, sound is wonderfully wedded to sense here and this is a book which yields up in richness what I most long for when I pick up a book of poems: vision; experience; travel in the world as another soul views it. That is the primary function of all literature, it seems to me—the

2

simplest and one of the holiest transactions in the world, the *companionship* of writer and reader. Rick Wilson is a good companion. Welcome to his world. Read slowly and travel well, enjoy the view.

Richard Bausch
Fairfax, Virginia
January 1988

For my family...Mom and Dad
my Franciscan brothers
my students
and always, Carolyn
who see me through

I. BENEDICTIONS

"I have nothing to ask a blessing for,
except these words."

James Wright

BENEDICTION

("St. Anthony went to the mouth of the river by
the sea, and began to call the fishes in God's
name.")
Little Flowers of St. Francis

Evening genuflects,
While I kneel at the creek's edge
Watching bluegill rise to tossed petals,
Wanting to write words, right as rain
Smooth as skipped stones—
And release them when the aim
And balance are right.
Fish rising to the rings of forever
As they must have done
To the poor man of Padua's blessing,
While gathering prayers in the dark.

7

BEERCANNUS americanus

You can find it
where the pocked faces
of NO HUNTING signs
stare dimly
from the fenceposts
leaning into autumnal shadow,
where a boy with a .22
once skittered
a Schlitz can up
the path,
his only kill
bullet-ridden
and bent,
hardly noticed now
amid the oak leaf litter;
so rich with loam
and the dark power
of moist duff
that mushrooms emerge,
fashioned like ears
pressed to the cool
forest canopy.
Listening closely,
they might hear
a chamber being loaded,
the silence
taking aim.
Pointblank.
Dead center.

SCARECROW'S DREAM

A burlap vision
of fallow stalks
that spear and
stubble the furrows
now rusted
huddled hayricks,
whispering intimations.

Smashed pumpkins
puckered to
cruel air,
even the sky
corncrib dry,
where a seedless
wind snags
like barbed wire
and from the field's
frayed edge: a 12
gauge blast.

A crow
    caws
     caws
      caws
its wings sweeping
at the sunset
with the scythe of song.

Frost etching
your paned landscape
(boundaried by split-
rail fences)

then a warm handprint
melting it to clarity,
twilight's kneeling
shadow nuzzles
the cold glass
and reflected back
is a daguerreotype
plate of your face.

Smoke whisps
from a woodburning
cookstove:
slow vapor-breath
of grazing Herefords
curls.

Impaled upon a bent nail:
swatches of denim
sleeve flail
wildly with every
gust: bits of broom
and newsprint are winnowed
to the earth
heaved clods

and while calling
the tassel-haired
young ones home,
his broomstick spine
shivers
right down
to the grain.

32° AND DROPPING

my pockets
empty milkweed pods

wind-ridge eyes
red as sumac

picking Beggar Lice
off my jeans,
I want to know
what the touchstones hold:
waiting
in the cold

I ask
of tossed bones,
entrails and floating oil

but find
only the sheltered
shingles of the pine
cones

their brittle
shadows
the crow and Turkey hawk

peppered
so sparse

this hoarfrost
November

WINTER PRELUDE

leaves strewn
at your feet
like a shredded
pinata:
stabbed,
ripped by
the Wind-child
impatient for
the fiesta
to end,
so he
stuffs his pockets
full of solar
confetti and
saunters home
whistling all the way.

QUIET CAVE POEM
(after Robert Francis)

Ned's Mountain rockmoss	boundarystones vinetangle	foot-trail cavemouth
crawlway petre-dirt	carbide cutknees	coolblack bellycrawl
mudprint brownbats	breath-echoes flowstone	cavecrickets graffitti
beercan drip	stalactite limedrop	guano drip
salammander slip-pit	ropeladder breakdown	snap-link fissure
spongework rimstone	gypsum-flowers moonmilk	waterfall siltbottom
rockclank shimmy-through	riffled-ceiling foothold	chimney-chute light-shaft
eye-squinting washtub	womb-wet bedsprings	sinkhole sun-stained boulders

Buford Tuttle's Pasture

QUARRY

So I spend most of the time attempting
to sort loneliness from solitude. Yet, here,
in the dusk, I know isolation for both
of us, the hewers, the chislers of stone,
for I have been staring intently
at these formations, these cracks
and seen the attrition that fingers
the textured, rooted rock
is patience, and have realized
it will make no faces but those imagined
in the cold sockets of looming grotesqueries

SUN DANCE

Sun Canticle Sun
paten bronzed
flamed notes

dew drying sun
monarch and marigold brushstrokes

clean motes of dawn
exorcize the cold

loud Lord
rayed swored

sparked with fiery presence
an anointing of light:

birth this day
as these open hands
offer

a quiet song
of awe, then joy

now bathe in the solar breath
of His Word:

AWAKE!
draw near...

NOCTURNAL BENISON

Night slowly resume
with the nuance of a voice
intoning, "Ecce, Ecce, Ecce."

Here a pale moth
flutters in upon
loam-fraught breath and alights

On one bald patch of stone:
so poised and dust lonely,
so sure of a pure presence

That it gently folds
its saffron wings,
thin and translucent
as a paper lantern.

It has relinquished the pull
to the light for this
benison, this moment

Burning with the soft blush
of shadow at every edge
and tremulous with its own weight.

Listen:
the soft caress of unknowing,
something
that almost hints at prayer.

THE GOURD DIPPER

"The gourd figures primarily in the story of Jonah,
when God made a gourd grow so fast that over-
night it created an arbor to shade Jonah and
diminish his grief (Jon. 4: 9-10). The gourd, sug-
gesting Jonah's reemergence from the whale, has
become a symbol of the Resurrection."
A Handbook of Symbols in Christian Art

Walk the fallow rows of the south
twenty until you find a gourd
picked ripe and thumped solid,
one that dreams the ways of
the water.

Hollow it out. Scattering the bright,
slick seeds at your feet, carving
deep as your thirst.
Scrape away the lesser pulp
and let the Barlow blade
shape the Earth element.

Now wash off the crust
of soil with your spittle
rubbing the rind
palmwise until it lacquers
smooth; glaze it.

When you string it out
to dry, have it sing
on a leather thong
eddy in wind currents
and gather strong draughts
to it.

And now, seek out still water
slight with silt and cold.
Dip and draw-up
the shards of your reflection
that spill off the lip's edge.
Here you are free to drink deep.

Let it quell the burning
Let it quench to the core

At last, imagine how long
that gourd-dipper took to find you
how many turnings it may take
before the next one rises
nestled in the dirt mattress somewhere,
somewhere out along the south twenty.

DE PROFUNDIS

An abandoned cocoon
anchors silently
in last season's bare Sycamore.
Its silk lampshade worn
gray and limp with dusk shadow,
as the wind's graffitti
clings to its thread loose tatters.

Sitting here, moth-lonely
tending ash and drink
my spun life is a frail lung
collapsed in the pale, thin branches
of my ribs.

Still there is
a breathing
too hushed to hear...

And somewhere
deeper still
some flutter-weary night thing
circles about my thoughts

searching for a halo of light
in which to ignite.

II. BETWEEN A ROCK AND A HEART PLACE

"Raise the stone, and there thou shalt find me,
cleave the wood, there am I."

The Sayings of Jesus
The Lost Gospel of Thomas

SAUL

"And immediately something like
scales fell from his eyes."

Acts 9:18

Snaggled in a net of light
with that lacquered glare,
the way to Damascus
blind-wise and straight

At the laying on
of hands
fish scales
flake from his eyes

His breath
suddenly fills with
crust-broken warmth
and the soft wet flush
from the lung's arbor

as lips part
to shape the Word
of his making,
the ever rising *yes*
lifts on stems, eyelash delicate

Releasing
into daylight
a deep slow stain
on the air

Gathering
a largesse of its own

BETWEEN A ROCK AND A HEART PLACE
(St. Bernardine's Monastery, 1982)

Flies spatter like hot grease
against the screen that renders
the world pollen-fine and pointillist.

Outside the monastery window
midsummer heat hangs
heavy as a confessional curtain on Saturday.

The earth leaks warmth,
spilled bourbon on a tattered trouser of road.
The air blisters with creosote

And skunk along the rail ties.
Beyond the glebe, the orans Virgin waits
in a silent pool of thistle and thorn.

A web over her plaster face,
an orbweaver broods upon the snagged
intrusion of samara seed

Suspended in wet strands of light,
quiet as the wings
of Van Eyck's angels.

High in this small bedroom
I drift off in a screed of shadow
the color of hot leaves.

When I leave
there is this bruised knot
that remains inside of me.

Suddenly, my kingdom begins
here, now, in these bones,
this flesh, these palms

Holding nothing.

COMPLINE

("He walks everywhere incognito. And the real
labor is to attend. In fact, to come awake.
Still more, to remain awake.")
                                    C.S. LEWIS

The mountains' frayed edges
lose themselves
in weathered burlap

tarnished bronze of the earth's
paten
whose darkness
surrounds the solitary glow
of the votive lights

the friars' canticle walks
across
this boundaried land
searching

for some star
to steer this stillness
home

and nowhere
to shelter
the vernicle of their hands.

GRANULOMA

There and there
and there.
It's all happening
again.

Alone at the edge
of an open wound,
entrails gnawing
from the inside
out: an uncoiled
cottonmouth rears-up.

Fluoroscopic shadows.
Cobblestoned.
A stringline
to garotte
from the center.

In the palm
of night
a stigmata or
tatoo emerges,
staining my bed,
my taut sheets
that swell
with uneasy warmth.

My corrupt cells,
condemned inmates,
claw their way out.

And ricocheting
like a dirty joke,
they whisper
to one another:
"Tonight's the night,
pass it down."

THE ALCHEMY OF PAIN
(for Giles)

Pain
is a chastening thing.
It invents its own language.
You too will know its purity,
        its unclouded nature
        in due time.

A great
primitive howl of vowel
and diphthong. This kind
of pain knows no consonants.
        You long to curl-up
        fetus-like, a bruised fruit peel.

The surgical
aqua wall, scrubbed to glare,
has its subtleties, Hornet
needles kiss the skin
        with antiseptic memory,
        an inflammation of fear.

For the pain
of viscera is preoccupied
pain without theory. How
you want to rummage
        in the furnance of your body
        for the white, molten nugget inside.

Every needle
and nudge, you feel,
the way a lover feels

desire rise intensely to her skin.
    Frantic is the patient, and
    drawn are the eyes while

Nurses
walk briskly with their narcotic
keys jingling. Imagine, empathy
has its reasons. Hospitals
    aren't run without it.
    This is unconsecrated ground.

The hours
are not the same;
as if underwater, the pallid light
is different—a tedious difference
    like doubt or vertigo
    perhaps.

Pain.
It knows no shame.
Think of the fox. He gnaws
the leg caught in a steel trap,
    cracking the bare bones between jaws,
    licking away the blood and fur.

Leaving
sad wound-tracks in the snow,
he hobbles from the trap, glances
back, eyes filled with longing
    at the pruned paw—
    its forepad raised in supplication.

Now,
poised with arms around knees,
study your own wrists,
the frown of past intimicies barely
    severed. Here deep scars
    have deep lives of their own:

Recollecting
a public display
of private emotions.

DR. SCHRAM'S LIST OF THE NAMES BY WHICH IT IS KNOWN

(Found Poem)

The daily disease
Three days
Once in three days
The fluctuating days
Three fever attacks within two days
Disease of the five devils
The one hundred days disease
Fever-chill
Devil's disease
The one forever recurring
Heat entering the body
Coldness entering the body
Quilt over the skin
Dumping in the belly
Tingling in fingertips
To get the shivers
To catch small chickens
The chill-disease
The veritable illness
The venerable old gentleman
The irresistable malaria
Blackwater fever

TIME ON ITS SIDE

Hunger crawls in a crooked line,
Hunger stalks from here, to there, to nowhere.
Hunger speaks in small mouths of rice.
Hunger counts backwards like a patient anesthetized.

Hunger growls regardless of its leash.
Hunger is a straw-empty cage of lies.
The lens of its stare ready to ignite,
Hunger sprawls patiently in the sun.

Hunger knows its whims, is terminal.
Hunger never asks, "Am I my brother's keeper?"
Hunger is sloppy, skin-taut and navel protruded
like a series of ellipses.

Hunger breaks no bones.
Hunger, nothing less than a corpse's other masque,
Is visible, lonely,
Consecrated with flies that hover like dirt angels

Praying over their victims.
And here no lilies smolder at the edges,
Putting on airs—
Hunger waits with time on its side.

POEM, LITTLE TAVERN
(for Peter Klappert)

All I need is a double
shake. I'm not particularly
suicidal. Just neurotic.
I have a poem.
          A 17 line
syllabic. It cost me
a bottle of I.W. Harper and a broken
dinner date. But that doesn't mean
I'll publish it. Christ!

The sporks in this place
are too plastic. A poem is exotic
and quick like a Chameleon.
I can hide it in my wallet, under my desk blotter,
I can line my hope-chest with it.

I know all the M.F.A. rationale.
A poem is direct. Point blank.
Those who whimp out prefer fiction.
          An anorexic poem
only 65 words.
You revise the lines. That's not suicidal.
It's not even narcissistic.

I left it at home on my disk drive.
I saw one like it in "Anteaus". We all
need a poem. To keep our crosshairs
on the mark. You can sharpen your
tongue on the enjambment.

When I'm through
here, having loaded my synapses,
I'll litter my brainpan with its letters.

EXEUNT
(A Collage of their last lines)

Turn your face this way, so I can see you.
Well, I must arrange my pillows for another weary night!
When will this end?
A dying man can do nothing easy.
You will find my last words in the blue folder.
Did I not tell you that I was writing this for myself.
Upwards! Upwards!
Agir! Agir!
Mehr licht!
Turn up the light.
I want to go home.
I don't want to go home in the dark.
It is so good to get home.
Mamma, Mamma
Get my swan costume ready.
Bourbon!
Lord help my poor soul.
I have a terrific headache.
And it's a long time since I drank champagne.
Strike the tent.
Strike man! Why dost thou not strike?
Either the wallpaper goes, or I do.
I have long been partial to the river view, Doctor.
Let us pass over the river, and rest under the shade
of the trees.
It is very beautiful over there.
This lovely thing peace.
I am seeing things that you know nothing of.
Rosebud,
I shall be glad to find a hole to creep out of the world at.
This best of all possible worlds.

Now farewell, remember all my words.
The play is finished.
Draw the curtain. The farce is over.
Dying is easy. Comedy is difficult.
I don't think I shall get over this.
Is it the fourth?
Flames? Not yet, I think.
Dante makes me sick.
Is it safe?
It is nothing.
It don't signify.
It is enough.
So this is Death—well...
Here it is at last, the distinguished thing!
Lot of damn foolery.

ACT OF CONTRITION

Oh my God   I am contritely sorry
  for   even the sun
  skirts   this morning's clouds and
  I de   test all my sin
  whose   red heart blooms
  astound   ingly through my coat
  because   I dread the loss
  of a gift   a love gift, by the sky
  pains   utterly unasked for
  but most   of all because
  they offend   your igniting eyes
  snuff   ed to a halt, my
        dulled God

  palely, flami   ly who art all mouth
        and
  deserving   of all my love
  I firmly resolve with the help of
        monoxide

  and grace   to cry open
  in a forest   of frost, to do
        penance
  in a dawn of corn flowers and
        ammend my
        life

  to late poppies in October
  with   out end,
        Amen.

I.C.U.
(for D.B.W.)

Someone
deep in my marrow
is holding a child's hand
in an amusement park funhouse.
The floors are askew and
it's a tipsy walk.
Around every corner and
dizzy angle waits
just one more nightlight specter
to flash and fit
in mechanical macabre.
The narrow passageways stutter
back into darkness,
as we pass, from terror to horror,
from lycanthrope to decapitation.
And there is nothing to do
but cling palm-tight and follow
that laughter.

Waiting ahead
down another corridor
treacherous with gurneys
and metallic crashcarts,
a father shelters
a thin candle flame.
With a lost look
on his face, he stares
at his reflection
in the scrubbed wall tile,
(doubling his doubt).
Still his palm flickers

warm like an unspoken memory
he thought he'd extinguished
in the scumbling dark.

And for this moment
the air seems to listen,
holding its tapered breath
on the wick of recognition.

III.   HOMING IN

"I am a father of journeys. I remind you the dark
can be conquered by love-blazing fire. I made air
and wind a compassionate homeland. Be at home in the light."

Sister Maura

DOWSER

This hazel staff
notched with backcountry memories
        balances
my step across
            the pebbled shallows
giving of copper   citrine   mica-stars

while a deeper stream
        swells
from down inside me
        nourishing the moss quiet
            the frond serene
            these words...

RELIEF MAP 1:62500
(along the Applachian Trail)

Swift Run Gap, Hansley Hollow, Hansley Ridge, Elkton,
Pocsin, Death Mtn., Devils Ditch, Siloh, Bearfence Shelter,
Jollett, Peter's Point, Dark Hollow, Big Tom, Buzzard Rocks,

David Spring, Hemlock Cliffs, Spitler Knoll, Stanardsville,
Byrds nest, Stanley, Etlon, Cecil Mission,
Bushy Top, White Oak Canyon, Brokenback Run, Nethers,

Peales Crossroads, Keezletown, Shuler Island, Greenwood,
Athlone, Catherine Furnace, Ingham, Montevideo,
Penn Laird, McGaheys Ville, Newport, Alma,

Beth Eden Church, Lydia, Ashby's Corner, Kimball,
Vaughn, Fox Store, Mary's Rock, Jenkins,
Fairview, Shenandale, Jobbers Mtn., Thorton Gap.

OFF THE BACKROADS

A hubcap lying
in a road
    gully:

in its doubleness
it hands back
    the moon:

a saxicoline moon
so alluring with
    its spell of white erasure

out of pupate
darkness:
    a Luna moth

emerges like
silk from a sleeve:
    it circles then

alights upon
the convex surface
    drinking in

chromic radiance
fanning dry
    its veined, veridian wings

(the sound eyelids
make when
    they flutter)

and in the thicket:
concealed beyond range
     of vision: two

opal orbs
kindled with
     intent: watching
               waiting
               sentient

SEARCH PARTY
(on a variation by Rolf Jacobsen)

Your hand at rest here is a leaf
layed on in healing as it returns
to soft earth-rot,
and full of the dark breath of a hickory nut
as it waits in marrowed patience.

And I spy one who is alone
in these woods that stretch
from dust to dark soon—
hunters, good family men, who've primed
their ashen lanterns as they scumble
from ridge to ridge, then down to firetrail
and washout—swaggering through stone and bark
slapback as if they were searching
with kerosene jacklights, (faint as stuttering
fireflies spawned from small palms),
to make heads or tails of the faceless shadow
that trails a warmth all its own
or illuminate familiar eyes,
with a corona that cancels fear,
a suffusion that kindles grace:
somewhere promising
fire, food and sure friends.

BACK TRACKING

Saccharum amber
an ichor

from a love scarred maple
coalesing

Some wounds heal
festers slowly

only in the sacrament of seasons
cicatrice on the sore bark

with the changing
coming here again

of green-hued vestments
years later

to the liturgical
my fingers run over

dyes of Fall
her initials, braille-like

and though the Poor-will
lingering, a bitter-sweet balm

chants a litany of loss
then I remember

the Mourning Dove
this is what I've come for:

48

coos with arrival
tapping hidden sources.

LOVE POEM

Somewhere between
the sheet-sails
I navigate
by your eyes,
the constellations

We sprawl out,
the touch of you
cool and fresh
as spindrift

I settle into you
lost to the bermuda
littoral of your thighs

Sweet coral cove
between your legs,
that sandsoft
secret

And after you've gone,
night unfolds
from a conch shell

Then the curl
of breakers,
lips parting
in a voice
alive with salt

Promising your return
in the gathering white swirls
that trace my ankles,
then recede:
graceful as a woman
casual as the tide.

BROKEN SLEEP

(To Adam back the rib is plied,
A creature weeps within his side.)
Djuna Barnes

It's happening
again

my ear
against her chest

and I wonder
where my old rib is

echoing
in the spaces
and spans

of a cleaved
body

I was cloistered
locked into
this ice marrow
cage
no way out

though something
the size of a fist
shakes from inside

its regret
still muttering
in the dark

silence clenches
itself slowly
around my heart

till the beat
is smothered
blue

burdened
with loss

the thinner I get
the deeper it shows

POEM AT 2:17 p.m.

In the bottom desk drawer
the gun waits
like a man
in his room,
sulking and sulking.

The gun is made of blue-black steel.
It takes the hand
of a man to make
the gun bark.

Snatched
from the drawer,
the gun feels
sweaty palms on walnut grips.
It ponders this.
Its loaded thoughts well primed.

And somewhere
in the distance
a man in his bedroom hears
the leaden snarl.
He bolts upright.
With unmuzzled thoughts
now triggered, he cocks
his head to listen
as silence begins to puddle
at the window sill.

FAR FROM HOME
(for Helen Stepniak)
1892-1981

In the middle of the afternoon
laughter darts out of the t.v.
and circles about the room nervously.
Buffeting the pale wall prints and sallow tile,
it barely stirs the single strand of crepe
still hanging from last month's K of C party.

Again she's parked and poseyed
in the sun-stained dayroom,
her lap salted with crumbs.
Pockets swollen with wilted kleenex,
Pink slippers curled
like a still-born litter.

Above her, the wall clock turns
another jaundiced shade,
its hands murmuring with each
endless sweep.
She moves her lips,
but says nothing.

She finger traces the frail blue irises
that blossom on her forearm from last night's fall.
Gazing off across the linoleum,
the faces of grandchildren drift back and forth
across the floor like rain-stale newsprint
left behind for kindling in an abandoned house.

Its screenless porch door
opens and slams
opens and slams

THE ARCHETYPAL CLASSROOM

Done in late institutional cinderblock,
It is the English lecture and Chem. lab;
It is the detention hall and the homeroom
Where announcements are stuttered.
On the subconscious level it creates
A steady, uncanny hold. Thoughts come
Unbidden there, fingering all other moments—
In second grade as milk monitor, you watch
The wall clock twitch forward, cut to St. Rose
High and you're eye-tracing Shelia's breasts
And wishing it was summer. You imagine her
Glistening with coppertone, adjusting her straps
Ever so slowly. Another twitch and there's
That expectant lunch bell. You salivate on cue
Even though it's just fishwhich today.
Finally, cut to the last day of exams,
When you were part of a crowd and mostly lonely.
Just you and a Christian brother with coffee
breath
And greasy hair. Remember, the one with red ink
Running through his jugular?
Let it end here: the door left quietly ajar,
A stub of chalk sulks on the blackboard ledge
Nesting in its own pale talcum—waiting, staring
At the absence where the faces once were.

AUGUST NICHT QUALMS
a sequence

I. In the cul-de-sac the dry laughter of children
chalking in their sad silhouettes (mimes trying
to pronounce themselves). A shirtless jogger pads by,
out of breath, his face flamingo pink. A remore siren
circles in the distance and my wrist pulses blue
with traffic going nowhere.

II. Always the moths dance in silence
around the porch-lights: serialized stars.
Cars drool oil at the curbside. Streetlights
sputter like a synapse.

III. Offcenter, the moonwane mounts
over domino-rowed houses. The shadows it throws
deepen and distort.

IV. A leisurely tension between us,
our token smiles and my neighbor
pulls her shade on cue. Her T.V. aerial
begins its blank, languorous hum.
And I sit on the patio, stroking the cat,
stroking the dark. The ice cubes in my empty
glass shift and melt.

V. By now my cigarette ashes litter
the concrete slabs
scattered to the advancing
chickweed and clover.

VI. And nothing is draped on the horizon,
imprecise, until a fine sibilant drizzle

takes hold.
It anchors the stale sky
to the stale earth.
Powdered childscapes fade,
color runs to water
pooling in the cracks and clefts
of the cul-de-sac's walkway.

VII. A vague breeze sags,
down sidestreets
sour with macadam and mowed clippings.

VIII. Inside my sandal-slaps lead me down
the hallway to something empty
and bereft of air. With so few
dreams this curfewed August night
(the color of smoked glass on a vacant lot),
I know the incertitudes of sleep.

IX. Privately we empty our pockets
on the nightstands and dressers:
snared threads, worn change, remnants
of colored chalk—talismanic fragments
between body and mirror: behind the glass
darkly.

X. In cinders of twilight, I think of Didymus,
Thomas, before the wounded
touch. Unsure of his blessedness.
Just doing what he sees
by heart. Hand and heart.
Taking account and sorting
the persistent doubt
the balance of lies.

HOMING IN

The fireflies pulse faintly in the hole-punched
    mayonnaise jar semaphoring
        memories from a childhood soft
            with evening blush.

Sitting on the front porch
    alone, with the faint rumor
        of chimney smoke and bourbon
            my days have gone autumnal

flannel and thined out
    as simple as the bike path
        down by Kladder's creek:
            littered with the brittle stars

of sugar maple, the burnished tears
    of acorn oak.
        And there's nothing
            left to do but wait for the streetlight

globes to stutter on
    pole after pole and let
        the moth-battered light chase
            these insomniac shadows

out for a midnight walk ...
    My feet read the braille
        of the path I follow
            and the sharp footfalls of some

feeling still scuffs by searching.
    Always the stray sound of a dog

barking as it fends off
the fragile silence.

So I hum some fragment
of a song in sepia
a canticle of blessed
and bitter hours.

As I light a cigarette against
a faint slur of wind, my cupped
palms assume a stance
of devotion. I know

this melody: it ends
in prayers, petitions and
promises…the lost words
of a prodigal one sounding out

for home. No more than
a lost refrain to carry
me into the night, fading
in its own dream-time.

Notes

"COMPLINE" — paten: a plate on which the Eucharist is placed; vernicle: the sweat cloth of St. Veronica.

"DR. SCHRAM'S LIST" — The disease in this poem is malaria.

"EXEUNT" — This poem consists of famous death bed lines. The authors are: 1. O.M. McIntyre; 2. Washington Irving; 3. Ben Franklin; 4. Beerbohm; 5. Mozart; 6. Goethe; 7. Archdeacon Hare; 8. E. Duse; 9. Goethe; 10. O. Henry; 11. Van Gogh; 12. O. Henry; 13. William James; 14. Casanova; 15. Ana Pavlova; 16. Tullulah Bankhead; 17. Poe; 18. F.D.R.; 19. Chekhov; 20. Robert E. Lee; 21. Sir Walter Raleigh; 22. Oscar Wilde; 23.George Washington; 24. Stonewall Jackson; 26. Thomas Edison; 27. Musset; 28. William Allingham; 29. Citizen Kane; 30. Thomas Hobbes; 31. Arthur Brisbane; 32. Epicurus; 33. Louis Agassiz; 34. Rabelais; 35. Ed Gwenn; 36. Leigh Hunt; 37. Thomas Jefferon; 38. Henry Labouch; 39. Lope de Vega; 40.William Palmer; 41. Archduke Ferdinand; 42. Sam Bass; 43. Kant; 44. Thomas Caryle; 45. Henry James; 46. Oliver Wndell Holmes.

"ACT OF CONTRITION" — This poem is a collision poem combining the act of contrition and Plath's poem, "Poppies in October".

"SEARCH PARTY" — a variation of a poem by Rolf Jacobson, called, "Small Lights At Sea".

"I.C.U." is dedicated to my Dad.

"DE PROFUNDIS" — is dedicated to Ted Kooser.

"POEM AT 2:17 p.m." — is written with apologies to Rich Jones and his fine poem, "The Bell".

A Note on the Author

BR. RICK WILSON (Brother Didacus) T O.R. is a Franciscan friar. He was born in 1954 in Verdun, France, and was raised in Virginia. He is the author of a chapbook, OFF THE BACKROADS, (Hard Cider Press 1979). In addition, his poems have appeared in many periodicals, including St. Anthony Messenger, The Other Side, Gargoyle, and Poet Lore. He is presently head of the English Department and teaches English and writing at Bishop Ireton High School in Alexandria, Virginia. He lives with his Franciscan brothers at St. Thomas More friary in Washington, D.C.

ABOUT THE ARTIST

Shelia Keffe, a Washington, D.C. based sculptor/painter refers to her work as "Contemporary Icons". They are dark works touched with illumination, influenced by journeys in the East and visits to monasteries in the West.

Traditional icons use symbols to represent the spiritual reality of a person or event. These symbols are deep and timeless. They are meant to draw us into meditation on the world of the spirit. As in traditional icons, the figures in these "Contemporay icons" are made with few lines, simple shapes. The outer eye is not distracted by physical detail so that the spiritual eye can see the deeper reality. Icons invite us to gaze upon them. A sense of the shared invites the viewer to make them personal to one's own spiritual dimension.

Keefe's works are included in private collections, corporations and churches. Her studio is located in the Torpedo Factory Art Center, 105 Union Street, Alexandria, VA 22314. Her work may be seen in studio 339.

Scripta Humanistica

Directed by
BRUNO M. DAMIANI
The Catholic University of America
*COMPREHENSIVE LIST OF PUBLICATIONS**

1. Everett W. Hesse, *The "Comedia" and Points of View.* $24.50
2. Marta Ana Diz, *Patronio y Lucanor: la lectura inteligente "en el tiempo que es turbio."* Prólogo de John Esten Keller. $26.00
3. James F. Jones, Jr., *The Story of a Fair Greek of Yesteryear.* A Translation from the French of Antoine-François Prévost's *L'Histoire d'une Grecque moderne.* With Introduction and Selected Bibliography. $30.00
4. Colette H. Winn, *Jean de Sponde: Les sonnets de la mort ou La Poétique de l'accoutumance.* Préface par Frédéric Deloffre. $22.50
5. Jack Weiner, *"En busca de la justicia social: estudio sobre el teatro español del Siglo de Oro."* $24.50
6. Paul A. Gaeng, *Collapse and Reorganization of the Latin Nominal Flection as Reflected in Epigraphic Sources.* Written with the assistance of Jeffrey T. Chamberlin. $24.00
7. Edna Aizenberg, *The Aleph Weaver: Biblical, Kabbalistic, and Judaic Elements in Borges.* $25.00
8. Michael G. Paulson and Tamara Alvarez-Detrell, *Cervantes, Hardy, and "La fuerza de la sangre."* $25.50
9. Rouben Charles Cholakian, *Deflection/Reflection in the Lyric Poetry of Charles d'Orléans: A Psychosemiotic Reading.* $25.00
10. Kent P. Ljungquist, *The Grand and the Fair: Poe's Landscape Aesthetics and Pictorial Techniques.* $27.50
11. D.W. McPheeters, *Estudios humanísticos sobre la "Celestina."* $20.00
12. Vittorio Felaco, *The Poetry and Selected Prose of Camillo Sbarbaro.* Edited and Translated by Vittorio Felaco. With a Preface by Franco Fido. $25.00
13. María del C. Candau de Cevallos, *Historia de la lengua española.* $33.00
14. *Renaissance and Golden Age Studies in Honor of D.W. McPheeters.* Ed. Bruno M. Damiani. $25.00
15. Bernardo Antonio González, *Parábolas de identidad: Realidad interior y estrategia narrativa en tres novelistas de postguerra.* $28.00
16. Carmelo Gariano, *La Edad Media (Aproximación Alfonsina).* $30.00
17. Gabriella Ibieta, *Tradition and Renewal in "La gloria de don Ramiro".* $27.50
18. *Estudios literarios en honor de Gustavo Correa.* Eds. Charles Faulhaber, Richard Kinkade, T.A. Perry. Preface by Manuel Durán. $25.00
19. George Yost, *Pieracci and Shelly: An Italian Ur-Cenci.* $27.50

Forthcoming

* Carlo Di Maio, *Antifeminism in Selected Works of Enrique Jardiel Poncela.* $20.50
* Juan de Mena, *Coplas de los siete pecados mortales: Second and Third Continuations.* Ed. Gladys Rivera. $25.50
* Salvatore Calomino, *From Verse to Prose: The Barlaam and Josaphat Legend in Fifteenth-Century Germany.* $28.00
* Darlene Lorenz-González, *A Phonemic Description of the Andalusian Dialect Spoken in Almogía, Málaga — Spain.* $25.00
* Maricel Presilla, *The Politics of Death in the «Cantigas de Santa María.»* Preface by John E. Keller. Introduction by Norman F. Cantor. $27.50
* *Studies in Honor of Elias Rivers,* eds. Bruno M. Damiani and Ruth El Saffar. $25.00
* Godwin Okebaram Uwah, *Pirandellism and Samuel Beckett's Plays.* $28.00

BOOK ORDERS

* Clothbound. *All book orders,* except library orders, must be prepaid and addressed to **Scripta Humanistica**, 1383 Kersey Lane, Potomac, Maryland 20854. *Manuscripts* to be considered for publication should be sent to the same address.